SECRETS of the SKY CAVES

Danger and Discovery on Nepal's Mustang Cliffs

SANDRA K. ATHANS

M MILLBROOK PRESS/MINNEAPOLIS

Millbrook Press
A division of Lerner Publishing Group, Inc.
241 First Avenue North
Minneapolis, MN 55401 USA

For reading levels and more information, look up this title
at www.lernerbooks.com.

Main body text set in ITC Galliard Std 12/18.
Typeface provided by Adobe Systems.

Library of Congress Cataloging-in-Publication Data

Athans, Sandra K., 1958–
    Secrets of the sky caves : danger and discovery on Nepal's Mustang Cliffs / by Sandra K. Athans.
        pages   cm
    Includes index.
    ISBN 978–1–4677–0016–0 (lib. bdg. : alk. paper)
    ISBN 978–1–4677–2540–8 (eBook)
    1. Mountaineering—Nepal—Mustang (District) 2. Caves—Nepal—Mustang (District) 3. Mustang (Nepal : District)—Discovery and exploration. 4. Mustang (Nepal : District)—Antiquities. I. Title.
    GV199.44.N462M873 2014
    796.522095496—dc23   2013017736

Manufactured in the United States of America
1 – DP – 12/31/13

I am grateful to the scientists, scholars, and climbers who gave their time graciously so that the children who read this book can come to know them as real people, doing real things. The story of these dedicated explorers is not only a great tale of adventure; it is also a springboard from which children can launch their own incredible journeys!

To Finn, Cleo, Liesl, and Pete—whose spirit to venture into the unknown lures us to tag along. Thank you for choosing the path less traveled. And to my loving family: thank you for choosing the other.

To Peg: Thank you for the simple things, which are not at all easy to master.

I am grateful.

Vast cave cities are hidden inside these cliffs in the Mustang region of Nepal. Experts have begun to explore the caves and the ancient treasures within them.

CONTENTS

Cities in the Sky

ROCK!" Straining above howling winds, mountain climber Pete Athans sounded the alarm. He and scientist Mark Aldenderfer were perched 150 feet (46 meters) high on a crumbling cliff face. A section of the rock ledge they had just crossed had given way. Falling rock was one of many hazards in the weathered cliffs of Nepal where they were climbing.

Team member Mohan Singh Lama was standing below the cliff. He quickly moved to safety. The slab of dislodged rock plunged downward. It exploded into rubble near where he had stood just moments before.

Athans and Aldenderfer crouched low to get back to their work. They stepped inside a narrow cave opening—and got the surprise of a lifetime! The small opening was a doorway into a vast complex of cave chambers. They were all connected by shafts and tunnels. The entire cliff was a huge cave city that had flourished with people and activity more than five hundred years ago.

The spectacular human-made caves are perched high in the cliffs in Mustang (MOO-stahng). It is a former kingdom in the Himalayan mountains of Asia. In modern times, this tiny region is part of the country of Nepal. From 2007 to 2013, a team of scientists, scholars, mountain climbers, and even two children explored groups of caves in Mustang. Many of the caves were hard to reach. But once team members got into the caves, they discovered bones, mummies, manuscripts, and other remains of ancient human cultures.

Who carved these caves high into the cliffs? What purpose did the caves serve? What do the materials found inside the caves tell us about the people who once lived there? From their findings, the Mustang explorers were able to answer these questions and others about the lives of the region's early inhabitants.

CHAPTER ONE

The Land of Mustang

The former kingdom of Mustang is in the north-central part of Nepal. This country lies between India and the region of Tibet, a territory controlled by China. Mustang sits beneath the Himalayas. This mountain range sweeps across southern Asia between China and India. Mount Everest, the tallest mountain on Earth, is among Mustang's well-known neighbors.

Many people in Mustang speak more than one language. The most common languages here are Nepalese and dialects, or variations, of the Tibetan language. Some people speak Hindi, the national language of India. Others know Mandarin, the official language of China. Some people know English.

People in Mustang still honor a raja, or king. The modern king, Jigme Dorje Palbar Bista, is a direct descendant of the first raja of Mustang, Ame Pal. He founded the kingdom in about 1380 CE. Bista is a king in name only. He does not have any official power, but he is very involved with the community. The government of Nepal officially oversees Mustang.

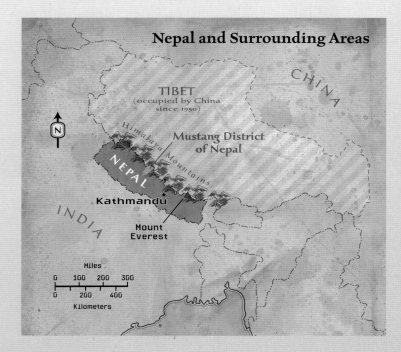

Nepal and Surrounding Areas

CHINA

TIBET
(occupied by China
since 1950)

Mustang District
of Nepal

N

Himalaya Mountains

NEPAL

Kathmandu

INDIA

Mount
Everest

Miles
0   100   200   300

0   200   400
Kilometers

The Mustang landscape is marked by harsh weather, rugged cliffs, and the towering Himalayan mountains. Most people live in villages such as this one, but hundreds of years ago, people lived in caves carved into the cliffs.

A Land of Extremes

Mustang is a region of cliffs, hills, and mountains. Like a water snake, the Kali Gandaki River twists and turns through the terrain. The rushing river water has cut a deep gorge into the land. It extends southward from Tibet through Nepal and into India. It is one of the deepest gorges on Earth.

Mustang has no superhighways and no system of mass transportation. Travel has changed little in the region since the 1300s. Most people travel by foot or on horseback. A network of walking paths connects villages across the 780 square miles (2,020 square kilometers) of Mustang's rugged terrain. In spots, the paths are winding and steep. Donkeys and yaks loaded with supplies step carefully across the narrow routes. In other places, the path is wide, level, and easier to maneuver. A 60-mile (100 km) trail borders the Kali Gandaki River. During the rainy season in Mustang, from June through August, the river may swell and flood portions of the trail.

The weather in Mustang is severe. The wind-whipped landscape is barren in many places. For this reason, the region has little topsoil and few plants. Mustang gets

To reach the Mustang caves, climbers and scientists cross a bridge over the Kali Gandaki River. In ancient times, traders followed trails along the river to carry goods between China to the north and India to the south.

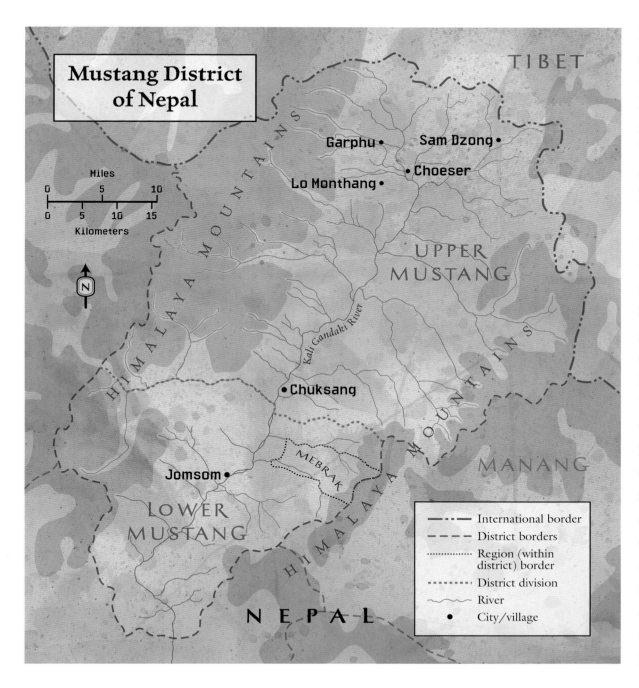

Mustang District of Nepal

TIBET

Garphu •   Sam Dzong •

• Choeser

Lo Monthang •

HIMALAYA MOUNTAINS

Miles
0   5   10

0   5   10   15
Kilometers

N

UPPER MUSTANG

Kali Gandaki River

• Chuksang

HIMALAYA MOUNTAINS

MANANG

MEBRAK

Jomsom •

LOWER MUSTANG

HIMALAYA MOUNTAINS

–··–··– International border
––––– District borders
·········· Region (within district) border
·········· District division
～～～ River
• City/village

NEPAL

heavy rains part of the year and is bone-dry during other times of the year. In winter and high in the mountains, the cold can be brutal. In summer the heat can be stifling. Mustang is a land of extremes.

This harsh environment is home to rare and endangered animals. Sleek snow leopards blend almost invisibly into the region's gray rocks. Snow leopards are clever and cunning killers. With masterful hunting skills, they easily outmatch their prey, which includes deer, rodents, and other small mammals. Snow leopards also prey on villagers' yaks, goats, and sheep. Colorful stories of these expert hunters fill local folklore. The bharal, or blue sheep, thrives in this mountainous region. Bharals roam in small

Horse Country

The people of Mustang often use horses for transportation. Some children in Mustang learn to ride horses before they can even walk. People prize and take good care of their horses.

The Yartung Festival, held every fall, is a favorite among horse lovers in Mustang. At this event, riders display their talents. They also show off their horses' beauty and skill. While mounted on top of galloping horses, at full speed, riders swoop to the ground and retrieve scarves. Also at full speed, they draw bows and fire arrows into targets. These and other stunts excite the crowds.

Mustang has few paved roads. So instead of traveling in cars and trucks, people frequently travel on horseback. The animals skillfully navigate the rugged trails along the rivers and through the cliffs.

herds and easily maneuver through the rocky landscape. Golden eagles and lammergeiers, a type of vulture, soar on the strong wind currents that blow high above the region.

A History of Trade and Travel

More than seven hundred years ago, many traders traveled through Mustang. They used a trade route that followed the Kali Gandaki River. This route connected with the Silk Road, a much larger trade network. The Silk Road wound its way from China across central Asia to the Middle East and the Mediterranean Sea. This network linked Asian traders and travelers to the markets of Europe. Chinese silk traders were the first to travel the Silk Road, starting around 200 BCE. Other traders and travelers quickly followed. Merchants traveling between China and India used the trail that followed the Kali Gandaki River. They moved goods such as salt, wood, barley, and buckwheat on large pack animals.

For centuries, people in Mustang have made a living by farming and raising animals. They raise goats and sheep for their wool, milk, and meat. They grow crops such as buckwheat and barley. In the twenty-first century, people in Mustang mostly farm as their ancestors did. They use hand tools and animal power. Flooding and drought are common here. People sometimes dig irrigation channels to carry water to dry areas and to drain flooded land.

Ancient Religions

Ancient artists made pictures and sculptures of Tonpa Shenrab, the founder of the Bon religion. Scholars know very little about him or the origins of Bon.

Historians think that in ancient times, people in Mustang practiced a religion called Bon. According to Bon teaching, a man named Tonpa Shenrab founded the religion many thousands of years ago. In the 700s CE, some people in Mustang abandoned Bon. They turned to the Buddhist religion. By the 1300s, Buddhism was widely practiced in Mustang.

Followers of Buddhism believe in the lessons of Siddhartha Gautama, also called the Buddha. He was born in the 500s or 400s BCE in the village of Lumbini, Nepal. At the time, the village was part of India. Rebirth—coming back to life in a new form after death—is a key belief in the Buddhist faith. Buddhists believe that a person's spirit is continuously reborn until it reaches the highest level of virtue. People achieve this level by living good lives and by following the Buddha's teachings. In modern times, most people in Mustang practice Buddhism, although some still practice Bon.

Race to the Top

According to legend, a great conflict arose when Buddhism began to compete with Bon in Mustang. The story says that two spiritual leaders, one Bon and one Buddhist, argued over which religion was best. To settle the dispute, they planned a race up Mount Everest.

According to the story, the Bon leader set out before dawn. He rode on a magical drum. Meanwhile, the Buddhist leader slept. Even when his alarmed followers tried to awaken him, he did not stir. He arose when the first ray of sunlight pierced the dark sky. He stepped upon the ray of light as if it were a path. Instantly, he was whisked to the summit of the mountain and won the race.

Another legend says that the forces of Bon and the forces of Buddhism fought a battle near the Marjung cliffs in Mustang. The Bon forces, led by a dragon spirit, were defeated. Legend says the dragon's intestines and blood spilled over the cliffs. They colored the cliffs red, yellow, and blue.

CHAPTER TWO

The Mustang Caves

The caves of Mustang are enchanting and mysterious. Thousands of them are scattered across different parts of the region. Most of the caves are in Upper (northern) Mustang, where our story takes place. Each cave was hand-carved by human beings. People probably used tools made of stone, wood, animal bone, bronze, and iron to carve into the cliffs and hillsides. The rock they dug into is a mixture of stones, clay, and sand. It is softer than many other kinds of rock and is not difficult to carve.

High Rises and Low Rises

Some of the caves in Mustang are nicknamed sky caves because they are high in the air. The entrances are far overhead—as high as the top of a ten-story building. The only way to reach many of the sky caves is by climbing straight up the cliffs. None of the caves has steps or ladders for easy access.

Rockin' in Mustang!

Many cliffs in Mustang contain richly colored minerals such as feldspar, tourmaline, and zircon. These minerals give the cliffs a variety of colors, including deep red, brown, yellow, and blue. In some places, mineral-rich springs trickle down the cliffs. The trickling water has stained some cliffs in northern Mustang a bright orange.

The dark circles in the lower left of this photograph are openings to cave cities carved high in the cliffs. Historians don't know how ancient people accessed the high caves.

A climber has attached a network of ropes to the sides of a cliff. The ropes are clipped to his climbing harness and help keep him secure as he scrambles to a cave opening.

Modern expedition teams use ropes and other mountain-climbing gear to reach the caves. Scientists aren't sure what methods ancient people used to reach the sky caves.

Many of the sky caves are linked together to form massive cave colonies. Some colonies occupy the upper level of an entire cliff. Some spread out over a huge area—as big as five football fields. Most colonies have between two and ten levels. Each level holds as many as fifty rooms. The rooms are connected by hallways, with vertical shafts between levels.

In addition to the sky caves, walk-in caves are nestled out of sight on ground level. People can enter these caves without using climbing equipment. Like the cliff caves, some of the walk-ins have many chambers connected with hallways. Some have walkways made from timbers and stone. These caves range from single-room structures to multilevel cave cities with many rooms.

Changing with the Times

People in Mustang carved some caves about three thousand years ago. They used the caves for human burial. About one thousand years ago, during a time of warfare in the region, people began using the caves as homes. Living high up in caves, people were safe from their enemies. People also used the caves for prayer and worship.

In the 1500s, some people in Mustang moved into villages with freestanding houses and other buildings. Others remained in the caves. People also used the caves for prayer, for grain storage, and as lookouts for watching for enemies.

Eventually, most of the caves were abandoned. People began to think of the caves as sacred spots. They believed the sites were home to Buddhist gods, goddesses, and spirits. Some caves were thought to be haunted.

Lucky Charms

In Mustang, hiking along steep trails can be treacherous. Hiking is even harder at great heights, where breathing can be difficult. Villagers and traders crossing high mountain passes will stop briefly and chant the words "So so! La gyalo." In the Tibetan language, this means "May the gods be victorious." This is an expression of joy and gratitude for safe travel. Some travelers also gently toss a small stone alongside the path. The stone honors local spirits who will safeguard the journey.

A climber enters a cave chamber. He sees that looters have already visited the cave and perhaps taken some of its valuable artifacts.

The Chuksang Woman

According to a Mustang legend, a woman was coming home late one evening long ago. As she passed cliffs near the village of Chuksang, some falling rocks knocked her down. She was badly hurt and unable to move. She cried out for help. The people of Chuksang mistook her cries for the wails of coyotes. She called through the night, yet no one came to her aid. By morning, she had died.

Some Buddhists believe that if people die in great pain and fear, their spirits become trapped at the places of their death. They cannot be reborn. Only the living can release the trapped spirits through special ceremonies and acts of kindness. Then the process of rebirth can continue.

The Mustang people say that the Chuksang woman's spirit has never been released. It remains trapped near the cliffs. For this reason, many people think the area is unlucky.

The Mebrak Mummies

In the 1900s, scientists and historians became curious about the Mustang caves. In 1993 the Nepalese government allowed a team of German and Nepalese scientists to explore caves in Mebrak, an area in Lower (southern) Mustang. Using climbing gear, the scientists explored a seven-story cave chamber. There, the team made an amazing discovery—thirty naturally mummified bodies! The discovery made worldwide news.

The mummies rested on bunk beds made from carved and painted wood. Scientists determined that the cave had been a burial chamber

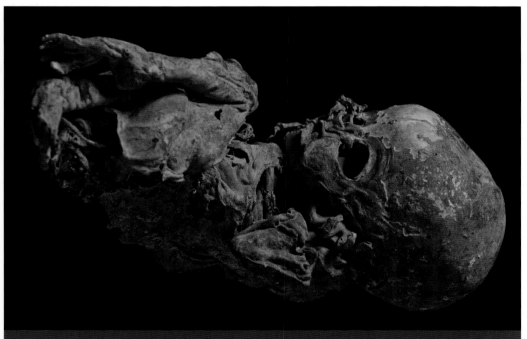

Dry air and cold temperatures inside caves preserved some dead bodies in Mustang, including this baby. It is one of the Mebrak mummies, discovered in the early 1990s.

Archaeologist Mark Aldenderfer studies a mummified skull discovered inside a cave.

between about 400 BCE and 50 CE. The cool temperature and dry air in the cave had preserved the bodies. In addition to bodies, the team found grave goods. These items were left with the bodies to help their spirits in the afterlife. Among the grave goods were pottery, jewelry, fur garments, a wooden archer's bow, and a bamboo flute.

The scientists also found the mummified heads of eleven goats and two sheep. The scientists found the mummified body of a horse too. These animals were probably valuable, prized possessions. The ancient people wanted to take the animals with them to the afterlife.

19

CHAPTER THREE

The First Expedition

In 2007 the Nepalese government agreed to allow more researchers to study the caves of Upper Mustang. The new expedition team contained scientists, historians, mountain climbers, and two children. Some of the scientists were archaeologists. They study the remains of past cultures.

World-class US mountain climber Pete Athans led the team. It also included American author Broughton Coburn, Nepalese archaeologists Sukraa Sagar Shresta and Prakash Darnal, and Nepalese team assistant Ang Temba Sherpa. US mountain climbers Liesl Clark (who is married to Pete Athans) and Renan Ozturk were also part of the team.

Athans had climbed Mount Everest seven times. He was even more excited about exploring in Mustang. "Caves aren't typical places to find Himalayan climbers," he said. "But this may be my greatest expedition." Liesl Clark added, "Stepping into the unknown is what interests Pete and me."

To reach the caves, team members left the village of Jomsom and traveled along the Kali Gandaki River. They traveled mostly on foot. Sometimes, to cross the river and to climb rugged mountain passes, team members rode atop sturdy Tibetan horses.

The team had a thirty-day permit to visit the caves. They had permission only to scout the caves and to photograph what they saw. Members were not allowed to alter the caves or the contents inside in any way. They were not allowed to remove any materials.

Finn and Cleo have accompanied their parents, Pete Athans and Liesl Clark, on the Mustang expeditions. Here they ride horses while other members of the team travel on foot.

The Dynamic Duo: Finn and Cleo

Finn and Cleo rock the record books as the youngest outsiders to enter the district of Mustang. Finn and Cleo are the children of Pete Athans and Liesl Clark. Finn was just three years old and Cleo barely eighteen months old when they went on the 2007 expedition. Since then, they have been on nine more expeditions.

Secret Cave Structures—the Kabums

Traveling on foot and horseback takes a lot of time, especially across rugged terrain. It took the team about nine days just to travel to and from the caves. That left only twenty-one days to explore the caves. The team members had to carefully prioritize their goals.

As a top priority, they hoped to locate sacred clay structures called kabums. Kabums are monuments built to hold sacred Buddhist artifacts and the remains of important religious leaders. According to local legend, seven caves containing kabums lay hidden in Upper Mustang. Some of the seven were said to be cliff caves. Others were said to be walk-in hillside caves.

Following a tip from a local shepherd, the team climbed high into the hills of Upper Mustang. Suddenly, Pete Athans and Renan Ozturk spied an opening to a walk-in cave. It was barely visible through the brush and rock. As they stepped inside, the cave's size surprised them. The cave was about one and a half times larger and taller than an average US classroom.

Athans and Ozturk moved deeper into the chamber—farther from the natural light of the cave opening. When they clicked on their headlamps, a jolt of disbelief charged through them. There, before them was a magnificent 35-foot-wide (11 m) wall mural—the size of a school bus. In the light of the headlamps, Athans and Ozturk could see human figures on the mural painted in black, red, and white.

The team discovered several kabums in the Mustang cliffs. This one had been smashed open by vandals.

Hundreds of years ago, artists created this detailed mural inside a cave in Upper Mustang. The figures are yogis, or Buddhist teachers. The mural might date to the 1100s.

An Ancient Masterpiece

Following the 2007 expedition, journalists flashed news of the team's discovery of the ancient cave mural. One report said that uncovering this masterpiece was "as valuable as uncovering an unknown [work by the famous Dutch painter] Rembrandt."

Italian photographer and art conservator Luigi Fieni was not officially part of the 2007 expedition. Working independently, after Athans and Ozturk discovered the mural, he went inside the cave to take more photographs. Using computer software, Fieni did a virtual cleaning of the photos. By studying photos, scholars have determined that the mural shows more than forty yogis, or Buddhist teachers. Each picture is accompanied by text that tells important lessons from the life of the Buddha.

Some scholars think the mural dates to the 1100s. They chose this date because the mural resembles artwork created by famous Nepalese artists of that time. "The painting is another example of the cultural richness of Mustang," said archaeologist Sukraa Sagar Shresta.

Deeper inside the cave, the explorers found a butter lamp. This cup-shaped metal lamp was designed to burn yak butter for light. They also found fragments of a statue of the Buddha and containers for food. The two climbers took photographs of the mural and the other artifacts without disturbing anything. This was not a kabum cave, but it was a tremendous discovery.

On the same trip, the team did eventually find several kabum caves. These discoveries proved that these legendary sites really exist. Vandals had smashed open some of the kabums with axes. Their contents were missing. Other kabums remained intact and contained cherished Buddhist religious artifacts.

Danger! Scouting the Cliff Caves

The team's next priority was to scout some of the caves perched high in Upper Mustang's cliffs. From centuries of weathering, the cliffs were as fragile as a child's sand castle. Climbing them would be treacherous. At any moment, the brittle rock could fall apart and send the climbers tumbling down the cliffs.

To make their climb safer, the team used hammers to drive long metal spikes into the cliff face. Some spikes were 3 feet (9 m) long. The climbers attached ropes to the spikes. The team connected their climbing harnesses to the ropes and scrambled up the rock face. The climbers drove in additional spikes as they continued up the cliff. More ropes were fixed to the spikes to create a ladderlike network up to the cave openings.

Even with the long spikes holding the ropes securely, rocks sometimes broke loose as the climbers made their way up the cliffs.

If someone above shouted "Rock!" those waiting on
the valley floor below knew that rocks soon would
come crashing down. They knew to scramble out of
the way. Climber Renan Ozturk described working
among the cliffs. He said, "As rock and rubble fall
on top of you, wind blows up [from the valley] below
you. Like [the *Peanuts* comic character] Pig-Pen,
you're in an endless cloud of dust."

On his climbs up Mount Everest, Athans had
faced frostbite, blinding snowstorms, and other
hardships. But climbing the cliffs of Mustang carried
different—and sometimes more extreme—dangers.
"The type of climbing we're doing in Mustang is
something no sane climber would ever want to do,"
said Athans.

The team scouted many steep cave sites. They
found different kinds of cave structures. Some were
small, single-room units. Others contained multiple
chambers. Some had been used as kitchens. Soot
from ancient cooking fires still coated their walls.

Other rooms had places for prayer. Some chambers were connected through a vast network of tunnels and hallways. Some networks took up the side of an entire cliff—like a giant cave city. All the structures had been hand-carved.

A Grand Finale!

On the final day of scouting, in an area called Marjung, the team discovered piles of ancient papers in a cave high in the cliffs. The papers were filled with ancient Tibetan writing. Team members could not remove the fragile papers. Their permit did not allow them to remove any artifacts. Reluctantly, they left the papers inside the cave. They hoped to retrieve the papers on a later expedition.

The team's glimpse into the past triggered the need for future expeditions. The discovery of the kabums proved the existence of the legendary structures. But what of the ancient papers in the cave in Marjung? What were they? Who had placed them there and why? These questions deserved scientific investigation.

In addition, many of the Mustang caves had already collapsed from exposure to wind and weather. Some caves had been disturbed by vandals. The materials inside them had been damaged, stolen, or scattered in disarray. Team members decided that the rescue and recovery of artifacts would be a priority for future expeditions. They wanted to collect artifacts and arrange for them to be stored and studied safely. For this, the team would need special permission from Nepalese officials. They would also need the expertise of additional scientists.

Climber Renan Ozturk organizes papers found inside a cave in Marjung. The team eventually got permission from Nepalese authorities to take the papers out of the cave for study.

CHAPTER FOUR

The Rescue and Recovery Expeditions

The first rescue and recovery expedition, in 2008, was led by archaeologist Mark Aldendefer. Pete Athans continued as the expedition leader. Joining them were Charles Ramble, a British scholar of Tibetan history and language, and Canadian Jeff Watt, an expert on Himalayan art and history. Kris Ericksen, an American climber and photographer, joined the team too. Pete's wife, Liesl, and their two children, Finn and Cleo, were on this expedition as well.

Roughly a year had passed since the earlier expedition. The team hoped the mysterious papers would still be inside the Marjung cave. No one knew what the papers were. But the team thought the documents would have important information about Mustang's past. Whoever had placed them in such a remote, high location must have believed they were very valuable and needed to be kept safe.

To get cooperation from the Mustang government, team members traveled to Mustang's capital city, Lo Monthang. There, they met with the king of Mustang, Jigme Dorje Palbar Bista. They talked with him about ways to preserve the papers. The king and other officials agreed to let the team remove the papers and other artifacts from the caves.

King Bista supports efforts to rescue Mustang's cultural artifacts.

Safekeeping

Every time the climbers prepared to ascend cliffs in Mustang, the lamas who accompanied the expedition performed ceremonies called *pujas (above)*. In the ceremonies, the lamas read from religious documents, burned juniper and incense, and chanted sacred verses. The pujas were blessings to keep the team members safe.

Next, the team visited a local *kempo*, a Buddhist spiritual leader. He, too, believed the papers should be saved. The kempo gave his blessing to the team. He also sent three Buddhist lamas, or holy men, with the expedition. Their job was to spiritually protect the team from danger and troublesome spirits.

Making Scientists into Climbers

Scaling the unstable cliffs in Mustang is risky, even for world-class mountain climbers. For Charles Ramble and the other scholars, the risks were even greater. They are not trained mountain climbers.

It was important for the scientists to study the artifacts and caves on-site. Context, or the environment in which materials are found, can provide important clues about a discovery. For instance, Aldenderfer needed to examine the high cave cities up close. Ramble had to see the Tibetan papers as they lay in the cave. That way, they could note details that might be overlooked if they left it to the mountain climbers to collect and photograph materials for them. "History is very important," said Ramble. "You can't make up the past. You have to look very carefully at what the evidence is. The general lesson is, don't take anything at face value and don't accept anything without evidence."

To make the climbing easier for the scientists, the team selected its routes carefully. It tried to avoid areas that demanded advanced climbing skills. "We tried to access the caves by the safest route possible," said Kris Ericksen.

The climbing was especially hard for Ramble because he had a fear of heights. But he said, "When you want knowledge so badly, you can't let things get in the way. My fear of heights was not going to prevent me from accessing that cave."

To help Ramble overcome his fear, the climbers coached him as he climbed. Athans guided and encouraged him with instructions such as, "Face into the rock. Place your left foot first and then place your right hand on the yellow rock by your thigh. That's it, Charles."

Library in the Sky

Ramble made a successful climb. Once he was inside the cave, he took a deep breath. An instant later, he was again breathless. Several feet from the cave opening, a thick carpet of thousands of written pages lay before him. Some of the text had been created with woodblock printing. Other writing had been penned by hand. Some pages featured tiny paintings. The pages glistened in the natural light coming from the cave opening.

The papers were in shambles. They were covered in bird droppings and had been battered by harsh weather. Some of the paintings had been cut from their pages— stolen by looters some time before.

The team collected and lowered the papers in a climber's haul bag to the lamas at the base of the cliff. The explorers sent down thirty loads—eight thousand pages in all. Once he was safely down the cliff face, Ramble and the other team members set up a field lab in a tent at the base of the cliff. There, they photographed and scanned the entire collection of papers. The job took hours.

Pete Athans *(above)* wears a mask to keep from breathing in dusty and dirty air inside a cave. Scholar Charles Ramble *(right)* holds a page from the Bon manuscript.

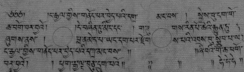

Ramble knows how to read ancient Tibetan. He saw that the papers in the cave were mostly from a single ancient manuscript. It contained information on the Bon faith. The lamas also knew ancient Tibetan. They helped Ramble translate the text into English.

The last page of the Bon manuscript *(above)* contained the colophon—with information about who made the document.

To learn more about the manuscript, Ramble and the others searched for the last page. They hoped it contained information called a colophon. The colophons of ancient manuscripts often list the name of the person who owned the document, the name of the scribe—the person who did the writing and printing—and the date the document was created.

Scouring the thousands of pages for the colophon was a lot like searching for a needle in a haystack. But to everyone's amazement, the team members found it. The colophon revealed the name of the scribe who had written out the Bon text. It also named the nobleman who had hired him to write it. But it did not provide a date for the manuscript.

The Bon Manuscript

Charles Ramble believes the Bon manuscript dates to the mid-1300s, when Buddhism became the most widely practiced religion in Mustang. Perhaps Buddhists wanted to remove all signs of their old religion, Bon, by placing the manuscript in a hard-to-reach cave. Or perhaps people who still practiced Bon wanted to keep their valuable teachings safe inside the cave.

When the manuscript was written, most people in Mustang couldn't read or write. But some men were scribes. They carefully wrote down prayers and religious lessons. Scribes used natural inks and pens made from quills, or sections of bird feathers. For paper, the scribes used a strong clothlike fabric made from a plant called daphne. They wrote in a dialect of the Western Tibetan language.

Art historian Jeff Watt believes that some of the ink in the manuscript's illustrations was made from silver and gold. The metals were ground into a powder and added to liquid to make ink. Several of the illustrations show Tonpa Shenrab. He is said to be the founder of the Bon faith. His name is in captions next to the pictures.

The Bon manuscript contains colorful illustrations, such as this one of Tonpa Shenrab, the founder of Bon.

In addition to the manuscript, the team found other written materials in the cave. Members found a book of proverbs, or wise sayings, and a manual for solving legal disputes. With the help of the lamas, Ramble translated these documents too.

Bones!

As the 2008 expedition drew to a close, the team had enough time left to scout one more cave complex. They chose a large, five-story complex near the village of Choeser. This time, instead of starting at the valley floor and climbing up a cliff, the climbers planned to start from the top of the cliff. They would lower themselves to the cave opening on ropes. The top-down entry would be easier and safer than a bottom-up entry. The team would not have to worry about rocks falling down on them as they climbed.

To reach the top of the cliff, the team hiked up from the side. They forged a route across less steep terrain. Then Pete Athans secured his ropes to anchors at the top of the cliff. Dangling high in the air, he made his way along the cliff face to a cave opening. He peered inside and leaned in for a closer look. Could it be? He took a deep breath

Sometimes it was easier for the team to reach cave openings by lowering themselves down from the top of a cliff than by climbing up from the bottom.

A Bone to Pick

Finn and Cleo think bones are cool. "Don't get spooked or disgusted by bones," says Finn. "We've all got them!" Bones help us move; protect our heart, brain, and other organs; and produce blood cells. Tissues called ligaments connect our bones into a single skeleton. The human skeleton has 206 bones. Finn can name all 206, and Cleo isn't far behind.

A human skull has twenty-nine bones. Some of the smallest bones in the human body are in the ear. The jawbone is part of the skull. It may contain teeth, which are made of enamel and dentin, not bone. The human nose doesn't have bones. The nose is made of a much softer substance called cartilage. Cartilage decays after someone dies.

The skull connects to the spinal column, which is also called the backbone. A human hand and wrist contain more bones than any other part of the body (twenty-seven in each and fifty-four in all). The strongest bone in the human body is the femur, or thighbone.

and grabbed a radio from his climbing harness. He knew that Mark Aldenderfer would be thrilled by what he had found. He said, "We have human remains!"

This was the team's first sighting of human bones. Athans had found a skull, a spinal column, and an attached pelvis. Shortly afterward, the team found the remains of three more humans in the cave complex. The scouting mission was successful, but it was time to wrap up the expedition. The team would return again to dig even deeper.

A New Team

Athans again sought permission to return to Mustang. Nepalese authorities granted it. The officials again gave the team permission to retrieve artifacts and any human remains they might find in the caves.

The team returned to Mustang in 2010. Aldenderfer and Athans were again the team leaders. Joining them were Mohan Singh Lama, from Nepal's Department of Archaeology, and Jacqueline Eng, an American bioarchaeologist (a scientist who specializes in ancient human bones). American mountain climbers Cory Richards, Matt Segal, and Ted Hesser would rig, or set up, the ropes and help the scientists.

Eng and the others were eager to learn more about the people who had made and used the caves. "Learning about new cultures, past and present, and being able to explore what happened to people in the past and give a voice to them and their lived experience—these are the highlights of research," she said.

Dress for Success
as a Mustang Rope Rigger

Mustang rope riggers and other team members need more than great skill. They also need the right gear. The following list contains some of the must-haves:

CLIMBING HARNESSES—Climbers wear harnesses around their bodies. They use clips to attach the harnesses to ropes or to anchors driven into rock. Climbers also attach equipment to their harnesses.

CRAMPONS—Climbers wear these spiked devices on the underside of climbing boots. Crampons help create traction (grip) on ice, snow, dirt, and rock.

DRILLS—Climbers use power drills to drive spikes and other anchors into cliffs.

FACE PROTECTION—Climbers and other team members often wear goggles to protect their eyes from dirt and debris. They sometimes cover their mouths with bandanas to avoid breathing in dust. Inside dusty, poorly ventilated caves, they might wear special masks to help them breathe.

GLOVES—Climbers and scientists wear gloves while handling human remains and artifacts. They do not want to contaminate ancient materials with their own DNA (deoxyribonucleic acid).

HEADLAMPS—Climbers and scientists rely on headlamps to provide light in dark caves.

HELMETS—Helmets protect team members' heads from falling rock and debris.

REBAR PITONS—*Rebar* is short for reinforcing bar. Climbers drive these metal rods into cliff faces and attach their ropes to them. The team uses extra-long, extra-strong rebar pitons in the Mustang cliffs.

ROPE—Climbers attach nylon ropes to anchors driven into the cliffs. They also use rope ladders.

Into the Cliffs

In June 2010, twenty-five horses, ten porters (baggage carriers), six horsemen, five cooks, ten climbers and scientists, and the two children (Finn and Cleo) set out to explore more caves. They headed for the Sam Dzong cliffs of Upper Mustang. In addition to human bones, Aldenderfer and the others hoped to find human teeth. The DNA, or genetic material, inside the teeth could provide valuable information about the cave people.

A climber examines a human skull from the Sam Dzong cliffs.

When they reached the Sam Dzong cliffs, Finn found a bone. He ran to Jacqueline Eng and handed it to her. "Hmmm. It's human—a humerus bone from a right arm," she said after quickly examining it. Eng and Lama soon found other human bones close by. The bones fit together into three partial skeletons. The scientists thought the remains had fallen 200 feet (61 m) down the cliff face from the caves above. They wanted to search these caves for more human remains.

While the scientists waited below, Athans and the other climbers scaled the cliffs. They dangled from their ropes, taking photographs, drawing maps of the cave openings, and making notes. Occasionally, the climbers would swing like spiders in and out of cave openings. "Our purpose was to get inside these caves for the scientists," said Matt Segal. Suddenly Cory Richard's voice cracked through the radio. "I have one human skull. No teeth!"

Moments later, Athans maneuvered into another opening and found what Aldenderfer wished for. "I have a skull with one intact tooth—a molar." Athans carefully wrapped and lowered the skull to the ground in a climber's haul bag.

Cave Carving

In a real-life scientific experiment, Finn helped archaeologist Mark Aldenderfer make a cave. "We wanted some idea of how long it would take to construct a cave and how many people it would take," explained Aldenderfer.

Along with eight villagers, Finn used modern metal tools to excavate a mini cave. The crew took more than two hours to dig out just one small cave. The early Mustang carvers used crude, handmade tools to build hundreds of much larger caves. It would have taken hundreds, if not thousands, of hours to carve out entire cave complexes. "The amount of time it would have taken them to construct the caves is almost incomprehensible," said Aldenderfer.

In two days of rescue archaeology in the Sam Dzong cliffs, the climbers collected bones from twenty-seven individuals. The team also found pieces of wood, along with animal bones.

No Bones about It

Altogether, in 2008 and 2010, the team found the partial remains of nearly seventy individuals. They came from four different locations, called tombs 1, 2, 3, and 4. The team also found skulls and bones from goats and horses with the human remains. The animals may have been placed with their owners for companionship on the journey to the afterlife.

Jacqueline Eng set up a field lab in Sam Dzong to study the human remains. Like a skilled detective, she pieced together clues from the teeth and the bones. By studying a skeleton, she could determine the dead person's height, sex, and age at death. By looking at broken bones and other clues, she could figure out what types of injuries or illnesses the person may have had in life. By studying teeth, she could tell what kind of food the person commonly ate.

For each bone, she identified and recorded important details. She noted where the bone was found, whether it belonged to a male or a female, the approximate age of the owner, and if it had unusual marks. Cory Richards,

who is a photographer as well as a climber, photographed each bone. His goal was to create a visual library to store digitally with Eng's notes.

The bones were mostly adults over the age of twenty, but some bones were from children. The number of males and females was about equal. Many of the skulls had fractures. The injuries ranged from small cracks to severely crushed areas. The fractures indicated that the people might have died in violent attacks or in battle.

Eng also discovered cut marks on about three-quarters of the bones. Some marks were barely visible. Others were several inches long. The scientists believe the cuts were caused by defleshing—deliberate removal of flesh from the bones—after the person had died. "The defleshing was surprising to us at first," said Aldenderfer. "We had never seen this and wondered why they were

Excavating the Caves

In 2011 American videographer Lincoln Else was seriously injured in Mustang. He had just finished filming Matt Segal climb a high cliff wall and enter a cave. He was planning to get his gear and join Segal. Suddenly a melon-sized rock fell from above.

"The climbers yelled and everybody at the base of the cliff moved out of the way. We weren't directly below the climbers, but the rock hit some ledges and sprang off to the side and ended up hitting me in the head," explains Else.

A portion of Else's skull was crushed by the rock. He was taken by helicopter to Kathmandu, the capital of Nepal. There he had emergency surgery. Else has since recovered fully and wants to climb again in Mustang. "It wasn't a climbing accident," he says. "I was standing on flat ground at the time."

doing this." The scientists think the flesh may have been left for vultures to eat. A similar practice, called sky burial, still takes place in modern-day Mustang. In modern sky burials in Mustang, people cut up the whole dead body and leave it on a mountaintop for the vultures.

Buried Treasure

The team visited Sam Dzong again in 2011. This time, Nepalese authorities gave the team permission to excavate the caves. This meant they could explore items below the cave surface by removing debris or by digging.

As they had done earlier, the archaeologists remained at a base camp for safety while the climbers ventured into the caves. "We were thrust into the role of archaeologist because the caves are so difficult to get into, and the scientists trained us to be their eyes and hands. This was unique!" said climber Ted Hesser.

At one cave opening, an armchair-sized boulder blocked Athans's entry. He peered to the side of the boulder and spied what he thought were jagged wooden posts inside the cave. They stretched up like fingers from beneath a pile of debris. As Athans shifted to get a better look, a torrent of grit gushed down from above. He dislodged the boulder and sent it crashing to the ground.

Once inside the cave, he switched on a video camera. Instantly, Aldenderfer was receiving live transmissions from Athans on his laptop. Athans began to carefully excavate the chamber, following Aldenderfer's directions.

Athans moved the wooden planks and other material out of the way. He crossed what was once the level floor of a tomb. Suddenly, he spied remains. He saw an animal

Pete Athans looks at a jawbone with teeth while communicating with other team members via radio.

skull—quite possibly from a horse. After removing years of sediment from the remains, he realized that the tomb contained much more. Multiple human bones—most of an entire human skeleton—lay in disarray among the wood. With the bones was a metal mask, the size of a human face. Everywhere he looked, Athans spied more. He saw the remains of a beaded garment, daggers and other metal goods, a large copper pot, and wooden cups.

Athans thought he had come upon the remains of someone of great status. The artifacts would be new and valuable clues for the scientists. From them, the scientists could learn even more about the early people of Mustang.

Discovery in Tomb 5

Aldenderfer spent two days guiding Athans through the excavation of the cave. The team called this cave tomb 5. The scientists determined that the jagged wooden planks had once been a coffin. It had held the skeleton that then lay scattered around the tomb. The coffin had been decorated with a painting of trees and a man on horseback. The wood to make the coffin may have come from an area in modern-day Iran, far to the west of Mustang.

Scientists think the skeleton was a local leader who ruled sometime between 200 and 700 CE. The painting on the coffin leads them to think the man was a skilled horseman. The mask inside the tomb may have been a funerary mask to cover the dead man's face. The mask was made of one piece of gold and one piece of silver, which had been hammered together.

Other artifacts from the tomb included daggers; a large copper pot; metal kitchen implements such as cups and spoons; and a three-legged vessel, possibly used for cooking. Scientists believe people placed these items in the leader's tomb to help him in the afterlife.

In addition, the cave contained a cloth tapestry decorated with hundreds of tiny glass beads. The tapestry might have been a draping for the human skeleton or for the horse skull. Like the wooden casket, the glass beads were not from the Mustang region. Some of them

Archaeologists use soft brushes and other tools to gently clean artifacts. The piece above was part of an altar, a platform used for religious worship. Tomb 5 held a trove of artifacts, including tiny glass beads *(top right)* and a gold and silver funerary mask *(bottom right).*

A Tibetan Buddhist lama leads his horse through the village of Sam Dzong.

came from India. Others came from Iran. The beads tell archaeologists that the people of Mustang did business with traders from distant regions.

More Visits

The team returned to Sam Dzong in the spring of 2012. This time, one goal was to continue to excavate tombs 3 and 4, work that had begun in 2010. On the 2012 expedition, the team uncovered more human and animal remains, artifacts, and metal materials. The team also discovered raw silk. The silk probably was brought over the Silk Road from China. This is a clue that early Mustang people did business with Silk Road traders.

In 2013 the team returned to finish excavating in Sam Dzong. They recovered additional human remains. They also found two more gold and silver funerary masks, similar to the one they had found in 2011.

Acting on a tip from 2012, the group also went into a region near Mustang called Manang. They had not explored this area before. There, they discovered a cave that had formed naturally. Deep inside the cave, the team found a room with hundreds of human and animal bones. The scientists will study these new materials to learn even more about the people of ancient Mustang.

CHAPTER FIVE

Digging Deeper

Scientists from around the world are very interested in the Mustang discoveries. The Nepalese authorities allowed the expedition team to send a few small samples of metal and paint from the artifacts out of the country for scientific testing. But most of the artifacts and remains are housed in Mustang. To study them, many scientists and specialists have traveled to Mustang. Experts have also looked at the climbers' photos and drawings and read their field notes. These resources form a rich pool of data for scholars.

Carbon 14 Dating

Among other things, scientists want to solve the mystery of the age of the Mustang artifacts and remains. To date ancient materials, scientists often used carbon 14 dating. Carbon 14 is contained in all organic objects—objects that are living or once were living. Organic objects include bone, wood, flesh, and shell. When people are alive, they take in carbon 14 from the plants they eat. When people die, they no longer take in carbon 14.

Scientists know that carbon 14 breaks down at a fixed rate. They compare the amount of carbon 14 in ancient artifacts and remains to the amount in living things. Using these numbers, they can calculate how long the carbon 14 in an ancient object has been breaking down. From that, they can figure out the object's age.

The scientists looked at many clues—even soot on the walls of caves—to figure out when people first lived in the caves and for how long.

Mark Aldenderfer and other scientists used carbon 14 dating to analyze the bones and other organic materials they found inside the caves. They even used carbon 14 dating to analyze soot from the cave walls. The soot came from burned wood from cooking fires. Since wood contains carbon 14, scientists could date the soot to determine roughly when and how long a cave was used by its inhabitants.

Strontium Testing

Scientists also learn more about the Mustang cave people by testing ancient teeth. Strontium is a substance that people take into their bodies, mostly through drinking water. It settles in tooth enamel, the hard coating covering the teeth.

The amount of strontium in drinking water depends on the local geology. Each region has its own strontium fingerprint. That is, different regions have different strontium levels in the water. Scientists analyze strontium levels in teeth from ancient humans. They compare the results to strontium levels from different regions. When they find a match, scientists know where the people once lived.

To determine when this person lived, scientists may test the carbon 14 and DNA from the skull. Strontium in the teeth may offer information on exactly where the person lived.

DNA Testing

Our bodies are made up of cells. These cells contain chemical units called genes. Genes are like a set of instructions that tell our bodies how to grow and function. These instructions are carried in a substance called DNA. We inherit our genes and our DNA from our parents. People from the same family, such as brothers and sisters, have a lot of DNA in common. More distant relatives, such as cousins, also have DNA in common, although not as much as brothers and sisters have.

By collecting DNA samples from living people, scientists can determine whether those people are related to one another. Scientists can also collect DNA from ancient bones, teeth, and other body parts to determine whether ancient people were related. Mustang team member Christina Warinner is a US geneticist. She studies how traits are passed on from parents to children by DNA. She is studying ancient DNA from Sam Dzong tooth samples. The information helps her create a genetic map of the ancient people of Mustang. The map shows how different groups were related to one another and whether they were related to people in nearby regions. Warinner also looks at DNA patterns to track how groups of related people moved across southern Asia and the high Himalayan mountains. She can even tell if they intermarried with other groups.

Scientists look for broken bones, crushed skulls, and other clues to determine whether people died violently.

Connecting the Dots

Often scholars date ancient artifacts by comparing them to other artifacts for which they already have dates. For instance, some scholars think the Mustang cave mural was made in the 1100s because it resembles work by Nepalese artists of that century.

US archaeologist Holley Moyes studies the pottery pieces found in the Mustang caves. She examines the pottery to learn how the pieces were crafted. She looks for finger marks that show how the pottery was pinched into shape. Even the thickness of the pottery pieces provides useful clues to how they were made. "We look at everything: the shape of the vessel, its size, if there are handles—even small ones," she explains. If Moyes knows how the pottery was made, she can date it to time periods when certain crafting methods were common.

Giovanni Massa, an Italian metallurgist, studies the metal funerary mask and other metal artifacts from tomb 5 in Sam Dzong. Like Moyes, he examines how pieces were crafted. From this information, he can date them according to when certain crafting methods were used.

The team found a number of clay vessels inside the caves. Studying the pieces carefully provides clues to date the pottery.

Dr. Eng's Field Laboratory

The equipment in bioarchaeologist Jacqueline Eng's field laboratory includes these tools:

- Paper forms for recording data, pens and pencils, cameras and other photography equipment, computer equipment, and dental kits to make molds of human teeth
- Calipers (which are like tweezers) for measuring the thickness of objects, measuring tapes, rulers, and metric graph paper
- Magnifying glasses and digital microscopes for observation

Eng's process includes these steps:

- She gently cleans bones and teeth using brushes. If the materials are not too fragile, she also cleans them with water.
- She identifies bones and the age and sex of the individuals they come from.
- She uses a magnifying loupe, or glass, to enlarge small objects to thirty times their actual size.
- She uses a handheld digital microscope to photograph and measure bones. It shines a small, very focused, and intense light beam onto small bone surfaces. The photographs reveal important details about the bones.
- Eng feels the bones with her hands to note their shape and to detect unusual features.

New Theories

Carbon 14 and other dating methods helped scientists determine that several different groups used the Mustang caves over time. The earliest caves were carved about three thousand years ago. They were burial chambers. They were not made to be lived in.

Around one thousand years ago, people began to take shelter in the caves. Historians think this was a time of great conflict in the Himalayan region. Different groups fought for control of the Kali Gandaki River valley and the trade route along the river. Living high up in cliffs, people were safe from battles and intruders. They could keep watch from the wooden walkways they built outside cave entrances. If danger approached, they could retreat inside the cave complexes for protection. Scientists think they may have covered cave openings with rock shields. Inside, residents had cooking hearths, stone containers for storing grain, clay vessels, and other belongings.

Historians know that in the 1500s, people in Mustang started moving into villages. Some people still lived in the caves, but most caves became places of quiet prayer, meditation, and retreat. Others were used to store grain and the grasses that villagers fed to their animals.

Several families live in these cave dwellings in the village of Choeser.

Modern Uses

In the Upper Mustang villages of Choeser and Garphu, a few people still use caves as homes. Living in a cave can be tough, however. The caves don't have electricity or running water. Some people use caves for long meditation sessions. They live in caves for up to a month at a time. During the month, they pray and seek enlightenment, or spiritual awakening. Others use caves to store grains such as wheat, barley, and buckwheat during harvesttime in October.

Preservation of Artifacts

The expedition team, the people of Mustang, and the government of Nepal have taken great care to safeguard and preserve items from the Mustang caves. Most of the artifacts have been placed in a museum for safety and display. Most of the human remains are stored in other facilities in Mustang. Nearby residents monitor the site containing the cave mural. They have built protective enclosures to keep the mural safe.

The Bon manuscript and other documents retrieved from the cave in Marjung are stored in a Buddhist monastery (religious center) in the village of Lo Monthang. Charles Ramble continues to study and translate the texts. He works with lamas, Nepalese scholars, and scholars from abroad. Students of religion from around the world have come to Lo Monthang to study the Bon manuscript.

A lama visits the Mustang cave mural. Local residents make sure the mural is kept safe from harm.

Many of the scientific studies of the Mustang artifacts and remains are ongoing. Some studies will take several years to complete.

Secrets Remain

Many mysteries still linger. For example, archaeologists don't know how ancient people accessed the caves. Scientists think early peoples might have used wooden ladders or pegs to scale the cliffs to reach the caves. Or they might have dug out foot- and handholds. No one knows for sure, and the evidence is not there to tell us. Any foot- or handholds would have worn away over time. And if people used wooden ladders, these were likely reused to build houses once people stopped living in the caves.

The team's permit to explore the caves expires in 2015. Before then, the team hopes to return to Mustang to unlock more secrets. Members of the team continue to work closely with other scientists to analyze data. Together they are shaping theories about the caves and the ancient peoples who carved them. The exploration team has uncovered treasured artifacts. It has also given us a richer understanding of a unique part of the world and its human history.

Who's Who?

MARK ALDENDERFER is an archaeologist. He studies ancient cultures of the Andes Mountains in South America and ancient cultures of Tibet and central Asia. He also studies patterns of human migration.

PETE ATHANS is the leader of the Mustang expeditions. He handpicks the climbers and tackles the dangerous job of rigging ropes on the cliffs. Athans has scaled the highest mountains in the world and is best known for climbing Mount Everest seven times.

CLEO ATHANS-CLARK is the daughter of Pete Athans and Liesl Clark. She was eighteen months old on her first expedition to Mustang. Cleo rides her favorite Tibetan horse, Doma (whom she calls Snow White), on scientific adventures.

FINN CLARK is the son of Pete Athans and Liesl Clark. He was three years old at the time of the first Mustang expedition. He has many friends in the small villages in Mustang. Finn works alongside the expedition scientists and scholars. He hopes to become an archaeologist one day.

LIESL CLARK is a filmmaker as well as a skilled mountain climber. On the Mustang expeditions, she helps Pete Athans make day-to-day plans, records the expedition's activities in film and in a journal, and does research for the team.

BROUGHTON COBURN led the early Mustang expeditions with Pete Athans. Coburn is a writer and an expert on Nepalese culture.

PRAKASH DARNAL works for Nepal's Department of Archaeology. He is trained in high-mountain archaeology and plays a vital role in the Mustang expeditions.

LINCOLN ELSE is a filmmaker and also a highly skilled climber. Else works alongside Liesl Clark, helping her document daily activities during expeditions. Else was badly injured in 2011 when struck by falling debris at a cave site. He has fully recovered.

JACQUELINE ENG is a US bioarchaeologist. She studies human remains such as bones and teeth. On the Mustang expeditions, Eng works in a field lab set up in a tent.

KRIS ERICKSEN is an accomplished climber, skilled at climbing in rock, snow, and ice. Ericksen is also a photographer. He helps capture the team's experiences on film, and he photographs artifacts.

LUIGI FIENI is a photographer and an art conservator, who restores artworks. He has restored magnificent paintings inside Mustang's monasteries for more than twenty years. He helps identify and date paintings and other artwork found inside the Mustang caves.

TED HESSER is an expert climber and rope rigger. He has been the lead climber on some expeditions and has helped excavate the burial caves in Sam Dzong.

Mohan Singh Lama works for Nepal's Department of Archaeology. He was eager to explore and excavate the high caves with the team of climbers.

Giovanni Massa is a metallurgist. Massa studies the metal artifacts found inside the caves to determine when and how they were made.

Holley Moyes is an archaeologist who specializes in pottery. Moyes examines pottery found in the caves to determine when and how it was made.

Renan Ozturk is an expert rock climber. He is especially skilled at climbing high crumbling cliffs to access cave openings. He is also the expedition artist.

Charles Ramble is a scholar of Tibetan history. Ramble has lived among the people of Mustang for more than twenty-five years.

Cory Richards is a skilled climber and photographer. He has photographed the Mustang caves and helps excavate and retrieve human remains and artifacts.

Matt Segal is a rock-climbing expert. In Mustang, Segal climbs into the highest caves perched in towering cliffs.

Ang Temba Sherpa helps the team with everything. He lives in Nepal and makes sure the team has supplies and equipment. He also arranges travel and transportation.

Sukraa Sagar Shresta works for Nepal's Department of Archaeology. He took part in the Mebrak expeditions in the 1990s.

Tashi Wangyel is the expedition horseman. He owns and cares for the horses the team uses to cross rivers, climb mountain passes, and travel along rugged trails.

Christina Warinner is a geneticist. She studies both human and animal remains from Mustang to learn about the history of ancient Mustang.

Jeff Watt is an expert on Himalayan art and history. He studies artwork found in the Mustang cliffs.

Cedar Wright is an expert climber and photographer. In Mustang, Wright films a lot of the action and artifacts. Climbing up cliffs with 20 to 30 pounds (9 to 14 kilograms) of photography equipment is nothing for him.

Timeline

ca. 1000 BCE — People in Mustang first carve cliff-side caves to use as burial chambers.

ca. 200 BCE — Traders begin to carry silk and other goods along the Silk Road, a trade route linking the Far East with the Middle East, the Mediterranean Sea, and Europe.

500s OR 400 BCE — Siddhartha Gautama, the founder of the Buddhist faith, is born in Lumbini in modern-day Nepal.

700s CE — People in Mustang begin to adopt the Buddhist religion.

ca. 1000 — People start to use the Mustang caves as living spaces, possibly for safety during a time of conflict in the region.

1100s — Artists create a cave mural in Mustang, with pictures of Buddhist teachers and with text telling about the life of Buddha.

1300s — Buddhism becomes widespread in Mustang.

1380 — Ame Pal founds the kingdom of Mustang and becomes its first raja, or king.

1500s — People in Mustang start to live in villages instead of caves.

1993–1995 — A German and Nepalese expedition team discovers thirty mummified bodies in the Mebrak area of Mustang.

2007 — Pete Athans leads the first scouting expedition into Upper Mustang. The team finds an ancient mural showing early followers of Buddhism.

2008 — In two separate expeditions, the team retrieves and documents ancient manuscripts from a cave. The team also locates human remains.

2010 — The team returns to Mustang and travels to the remote village of Sam Dzong. There, team members uncover a tomb with many human remains and grave goods.

2011 — The team returns to Sam Dzong to further investigate tombs. In a second expedition, the team discovers the remains of an important leader and grave goods in tomb 5.

2012 — The team continues to excavate the Sam Dzong caves. Team members recover seventy-eight additional human skeletons.

2013 — The team returns to excavate in Sam Dzong. Team members find additional human remains, for a total of 105 individuals, and two more gold and silver funerary masks. In a region near Mustang, the team discovers a natural cave containing hundreds of human and animal bones.

Source Notes

20 Pete Athans, presentation, Winamac, Bennington, New Hampshire, July 9, 2011.

20 Liesl Clark, telephone interview with the author, November 12, 2012.

24 "Secrets of Shangri-La," *PBS.org,* accessed June 30, 2013, http://www.pbs.org/programs/secrets-shangri-la/.

24 Pete Athans, e-mail correspondence with the author, September 26, 2012.

25 Renan Ozturk, telephone interview with the author, June 28, 2012.

25 Pete Athans, telephone interview with the author, July 23, 2012.

30 Charles Ramble, telephone interview with the author, July 12, 2012.

30 Kris Ericksen, telephone interview with the author, July 16, 2012.

30 Ramble, telephone interview.

30 Pete Athans, telephone interview with the author, July 8, 2012.

35 Finn Clark, telephone interview with the author, November 1, 2012.

35 Pete Athans, telephone interview with the author, November 17, 2012.

35 Jacqueline Eng, e-mail correspondence with the author, July 15, 2012.

38 Liesl Clark, telephone interview with the author, November 1, 2012.

38–39 Matt Segal, telephone interview with the author, November 18, 2012.

39 Pete Athans, telephone interview with the author, June 22, 2012.

39 Ibid.

39 Aldenderfer, telephone interview.

39 Ibid.

40–41 Mark Aldenderfer, telephone interview with the author, July 9, 2012.

41 Theodore Hesser, telephone interview with the author, July 21, 2012.

41 Lincoln Else, telephone interview with the author, November 12, 2012.

41 Ibid.

51 Holley Moyes, telephone interview with the author, November 11, 2012.

Glossary

afterlife: living in some form after death. Many religions teach that people go on to an afterlife when they die.

altitude: the height of a landform, such as a mountain, above sea level

archaeologist: a scientist who studies ancient peoples and their customs

artifact: an object remaining from a particular period in human history

bioarchaeologist: a scientist who studies ancient human bones, teeth, and other remains

carbon 14 dating: measuring the amount of carbon 14 in an organic (living or once living) substance to determine its age

colophon: an inscription in a book or a manuscript that gives facts about its creation, such as a date and the name of the scribe

dialect: a regional variety of a language

DNA: deoxyribonucleic acid. This chemical directs the growth and reproduction of living cells. DNA is passed down from parents to their offspring. Scientists can analyze DNA to determine whether living creatures are related to one another.

funerary mask: a mask placed over the face of a dead person

geneticist: a scientist who studies genes to learn more about human biology, diseases, and relationships among living beings

grave goods: materials placed in a grave along with human remains. Grave goods may include pottery, jewelry, mummified animals, and other objects believed to help the dead person in the afterlife.

kabum: a monument built to hold sacred Buddhist artifacts or the remains of a religious leader

mummy: the preserved body of a dead person. Sometimes cold temperatures or dry air naturally turn people into mummies. Sometimes humans turn dead bodies into mummies using chemicals and other materials.

reincarnation: coming back to life in a new body after death. Also known as rebirth, reincarnation is a key belief in some world religions, including Buddhism.

rescue archaeology: retrieving artifacts not only to study them but also to keep them from being destroyed by weather, looters, or construction projects

scribe: in earlier eras, a person who wrote down or copied manuscripts

Selected Bibliography

Banskota, Kamal, and Bikash Sharma. "Rural Livelihoods in Nepal: A Case of Mustang District." International Centre for Integrated Mountain Development, May 25–27, 2004. http://lib.icimod.org/record/22228/files/c_attachment_149_1535.pdf.

Blum, R. C., E. Stone, and B. Coburn, eds. *Himalaya: Personal Stories of Grandeur, Challenge, and Hope*. Washington, DC: National Geographic Society and the American Himalayan Foundation, 2006.

Bue, Erberto Lo, ed. *Wonders of Lo: The Artistic Heritage of Mustang*. Mumbai, India: Marg Foundation, 2010.

Marullo, Clara. *The Last Forbidden Kingdom, Mustang: Land of Tibetan Buddhism*. Boston: Charles E. Tuttle Company, 1995.

Matthiessen, Peter. *East of Lo Monthang: In the Land of Mustang*. Boston: Shambhala Publications, 1995.

Mills, M. A., P. J. Claus, and S. Diamond, eds. *South Asian Folklore: An Encyclopedia*. New York: Routledge, 2003.

National Geographic. *Cave People of the Himalayas*. Washington, DC: NGHT, 2011, DVD.

———. *Secrets of Shangri-La: Quest for Sacred Caves*. Washington, DC: NGHT, 2009, DVD.

Noel, Sybille. *The Magic Bird of Chomo-Lung-Ma: Tales of Mount Everest, the Turquoise Peak*. New York: Doubleday, Duran & Company, 1931.

Public Broadcast Services. *Mustang: Journey of Transformation*. Sausalito, CA: Mill Valley Film Group, 2009, DVD.

Sharma, M. M. *Folklore of Nepal*. New Delhi: Vision Books, 1978.

"Sky Caves of Nepal, Part 1: The Climber." YouTube video. 11:47.
Posted by NationalGeographic, November 19, 2012.
http://www.youtube.com/watch?v=WMTZBw1SISA.

"Sky Caves of Nepal, Part 2: The Scientist." YouTube video. 16:18. Posted by NationalGeographic, November 19, 2012. http://www.youtube.com/watch?v=kzu5JAgb2vQ.

"Sky Caves of Nepal, Part 3: The Photographer." YouTube video. 16:26. Posted by NationalGeographic, November 19, 2012. http://www.youtube.com/watch?v=01r7e7mhQ8s.

Further Information

BOOKS

Adams, Simon. *Archaeology Detectives*. Hauppauge, NY: Barron's Educational Series, 2009.
This book describes how archaeologists explore ancient sites and the tools and techniques they use to unlock secrets in the artifacts they discover.

Athans, Sandra K. *Tales from the Top of the World: Climbing Mount Everest with Pete Athans*. Minneapolis: Millbrook Press, 2013.
Pete Athans has climbed Mount Everest, the tallest mountain on Earth, seven times. This book, written by his sister, gives readers an up-close look at Mount Everest and those who try to climb to the top.

Cohn, Diana, and Amy Cordova. *Namaste!* Great Barrington, MA: Steiner Books, 2009.
This fictional book tells of a young girl, Nima Sherpa, in modern-day Nepal. Nima's father is a mountain guide and is often away from home on lengthy climbing expeditions. The book provides a good introduction to the traditions and lives of the people of Nepal.

Shrestha, Kavita Ram, and Sarah Lamstein. *From the Mango Tree and Other Folktales from Nepal*. Englewood, CO: Libraries Unlimited, 1997.
This collection of fifteen authentic tales gives insight into the culture and traditions of the Nepalese people. The book also provides information on the Himalayan region.

White, John. *Hands-On Archaeology: Real-Life Activities for Kids*. Austin, TX: Prufrock Press, 2005.
Written by an experienced archaeologist and anthropologist, this work teaches kids about the basics of archaeology through a hands-on approach.

Zuchora-Walske, Christina. *Nepal in Pictures*. Minneapolis: Twenty-First Century Books, 2008.
This book explores the history, the culture, and the geography of Nepal. Maps, sidebars, and full-color illustrations accompany the main text.

WEBSITES

Archeology for Kids
http://www.nps.gov/archeology/public/kids/kidsFour.htm
This US National Park Services site is great for kids interested in archaeology. Updated regularly, the site features exciting stories about well-known archaeological discoveries, as well as basic information for budding archaeologists.

Caves
http://www.kidsdiscover.com/blog/spotlight/caves-for-kids/
On this site, you can virtually explore a selection of naturally formed caves and then take a short quiz to test your knowledge. Created by *Kids Discover* magazine, the site features links to related topics and includes information for parents and teachers.

Dig
http://www.digonsite.com
This website is a companion to *Dig: The Archaeology Magazine for Kids*. It includes an archaeology glossary, fantastic facts, an "Ask Dr. Dig" question-and-answer column, and much more.

Nepal Facts and Pictures
http://kids.nationalgeographic.com/kids/places/find/nepal/
This website from *National Geographic Kids* provides loads of information on Nepal, including facts, photographs, videos, and maps. The site also has extensive links.

The Sherpa People of Nepal
http://kids.nationalgeographic.com/kids/stories/peopleplaces/sherpa/
At this website from *National Geographic Kids*, you'll learn about the Sherpa ethnic group of Nepal through the adventures of sixteen-year-old Temba Tsheri Sherpa. He is one of the youngest people ever to reach the top of Mount Everest.

Ten Cool Archaeological Sites
http://kids.nationalgeographic.com/kids/stories/history/ten-cool-sites/
This site from *National Geographic Kids* provides information and visuals on ten of the world's most fascinating archaeological sites. Learn more about King Tut's tomb in Egypt, Stonehenge in England, and the Moai statues of Easter Island in the Pacific Ocean.

LERNER e SOURCE

Expand learning beyond the printed book. Download free, complementary educational resources for this book from our website, www.lerneresource.com.

Index

Photo Acknowledgments

The images in this book are used with the permission of: © iStockphoto.com/pepifoto, (sand backgrounds) © Cory Richards/National Geographic Creative, pp. 1, 6, 10, 15, 16, 17, 18, 19, 21, 22, 25, 34, 36–37, 38, 40, 42, 43 (all), 44–45, 47, 49, 50–51; © David Stubbs/Aurora Photos/Alamy, pp. 2–3; © Kristoffer Erickson, pp. 7, 23, 26–27, 29, 30 (left), 30 (right), 32, 33, 48, 51, 54-55; © Taylor Weidman/The Vanishing Cultures Project, pp. 9, 12, 28, 53; © Laura Westlund/Independent Picture Service, pp. 8, 11; © Courtesy of Bon Shen Ling, the Tibetan Bon Education Fund, p. 13.

Front and back cover: © Cory Richards/National Geographic Creative.
Jacket flap: © Kristoffer Erickson.

About the Author

Sandra K. Athans wishes she could climb the Mustang cliffs and explore ancient cave complexes with an expedition team. But writing a book, instead, and being able to share this rich scientific adventure with children brings her even greater joy. In addition to writing, Athans teaches fourth-grade students, whom she calls her classroom kids. She lives on an old apple farm in upstate New York with her husband; two children; and the family pets, Toby and Bella. This is her second book about the adventures of her brother, mountain climber Pete Athans. The first book, *Tales from the Top of the World: Climbing Mount Everest with Pete Athans,* was published in 2013.